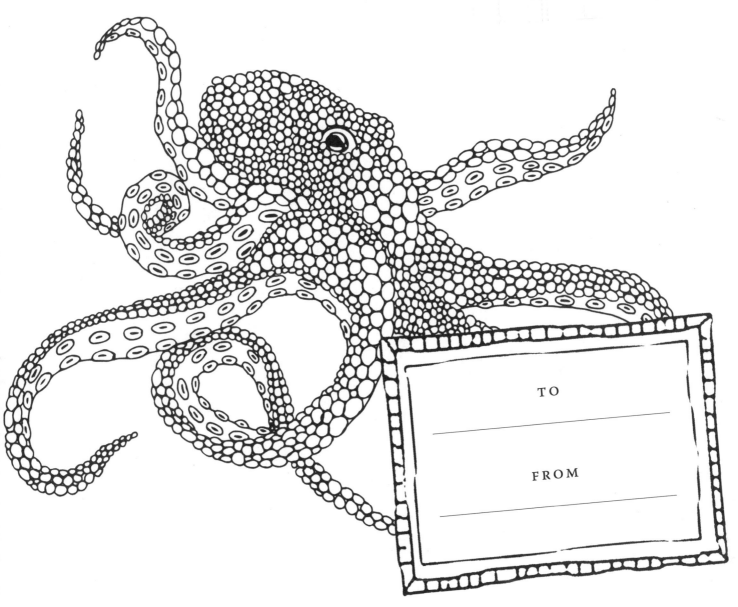

TO

_____

FROM

_____

KPT PUBLISHING

COLOR ME *fishy*

Copyright © 2017 KPT Publishing

Published by KPT Publishing
Minneapolis, Minnesota 55406
www.KPTPublishing.com

ISBN 978-1-944833-05-3

Design and Development by
Koechel Peterson and Associates
Minneapolis, Minnesota

Images are courtesy of Shutterstock

First printing March 2017

10 9 8 7 6 5 4 3 2 1

Printed in the United States of America

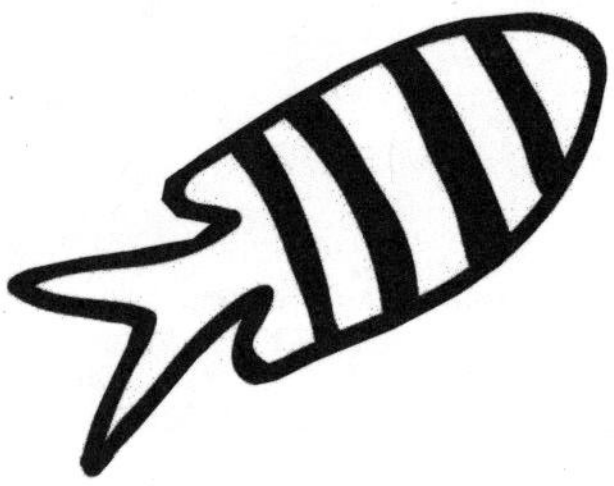

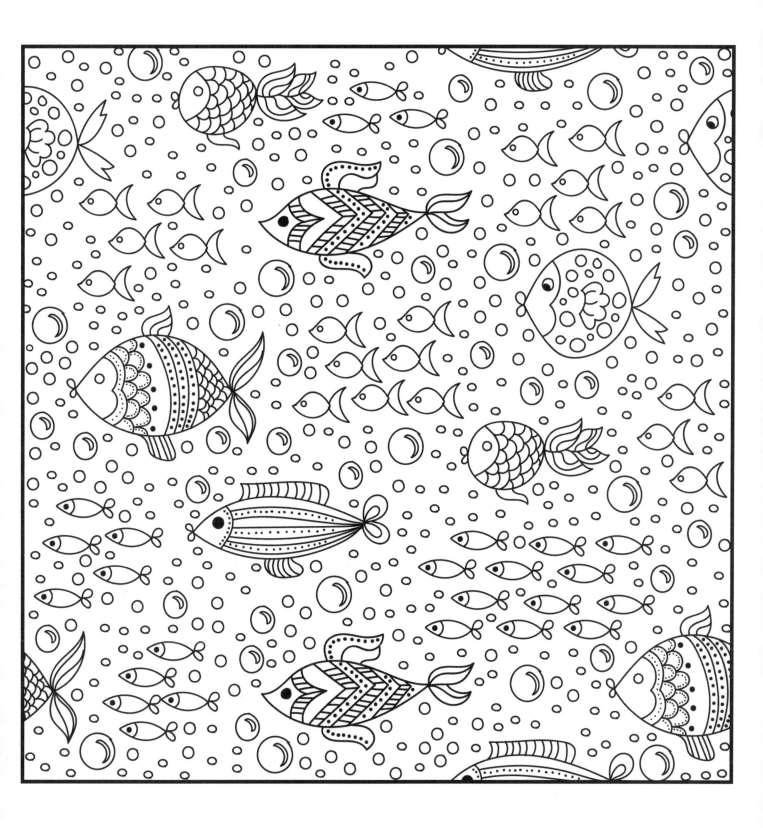

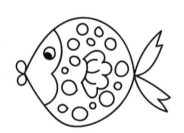

Remember, a dead fish

can float downstream,

but it takes a live one

to swim upstream.

W.C. FIELDS

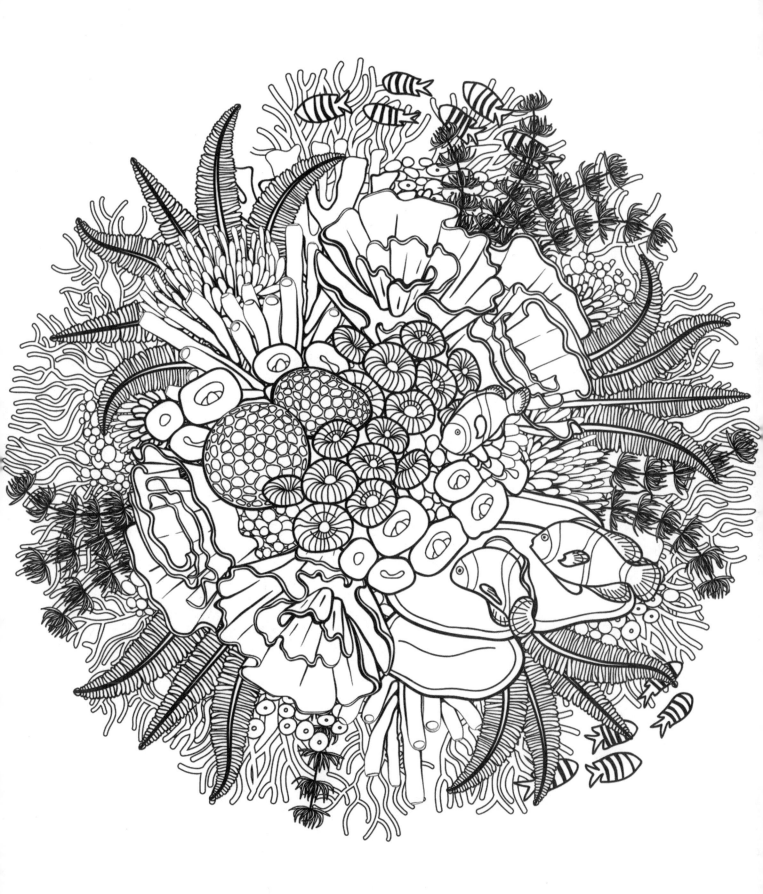

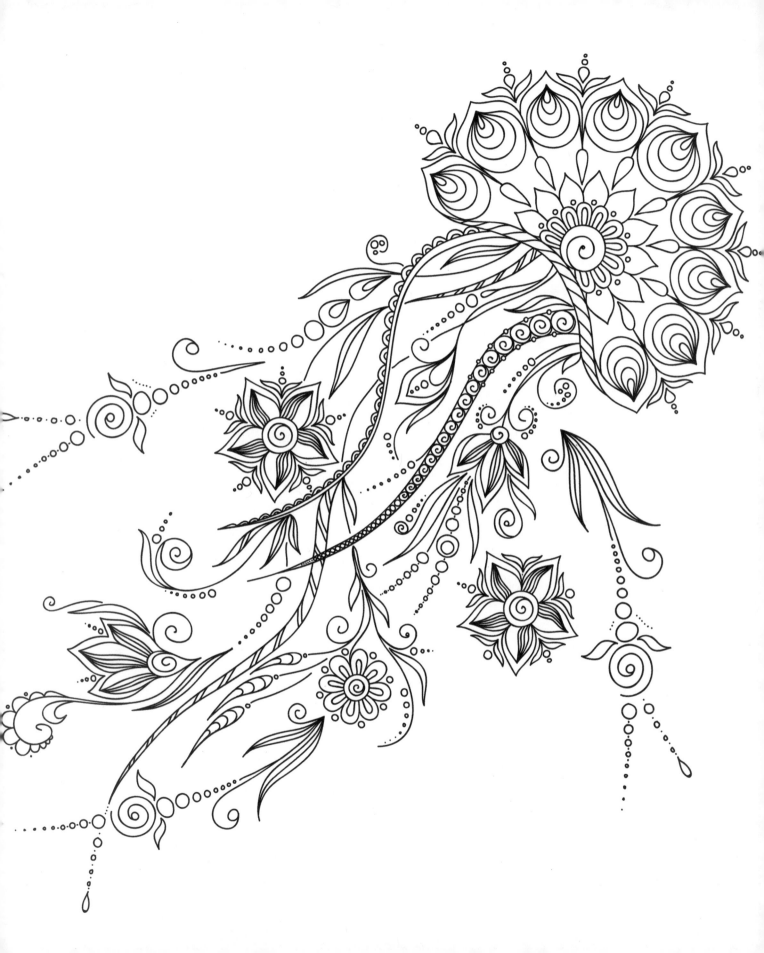

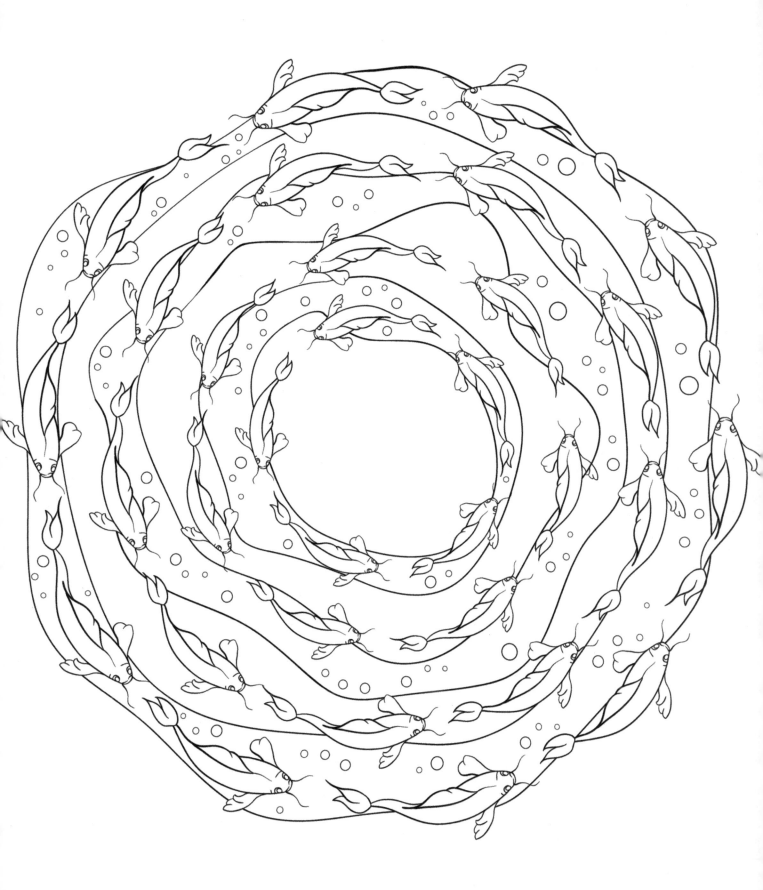

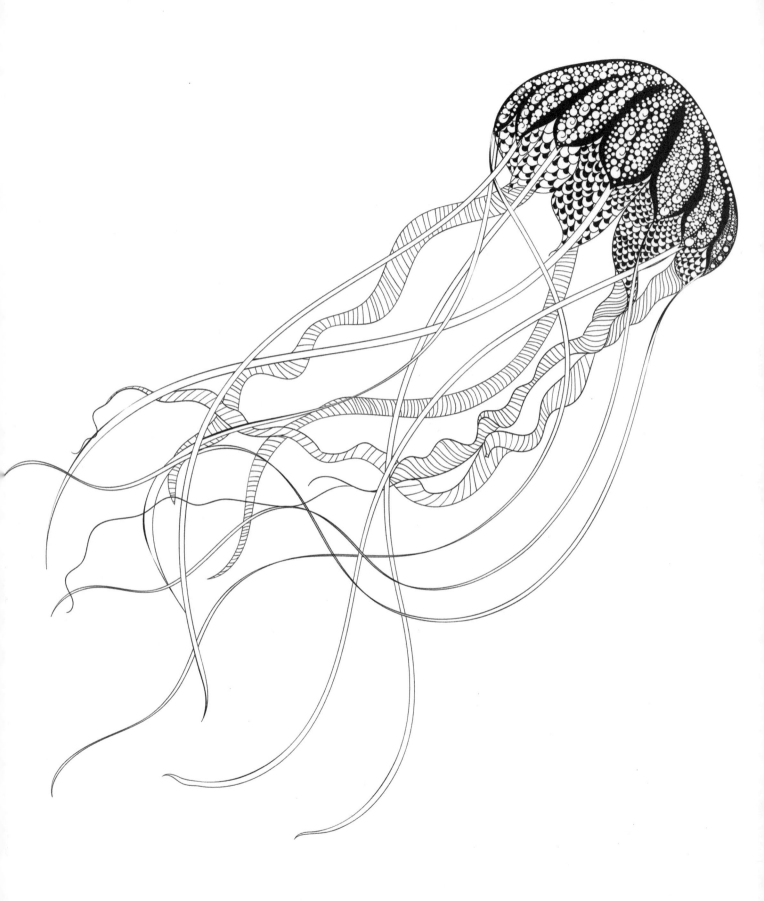

Did you know fish see more colors than you.

(A fish can see UV light.)

Come and swim with me
and see what I can see
in the sea.

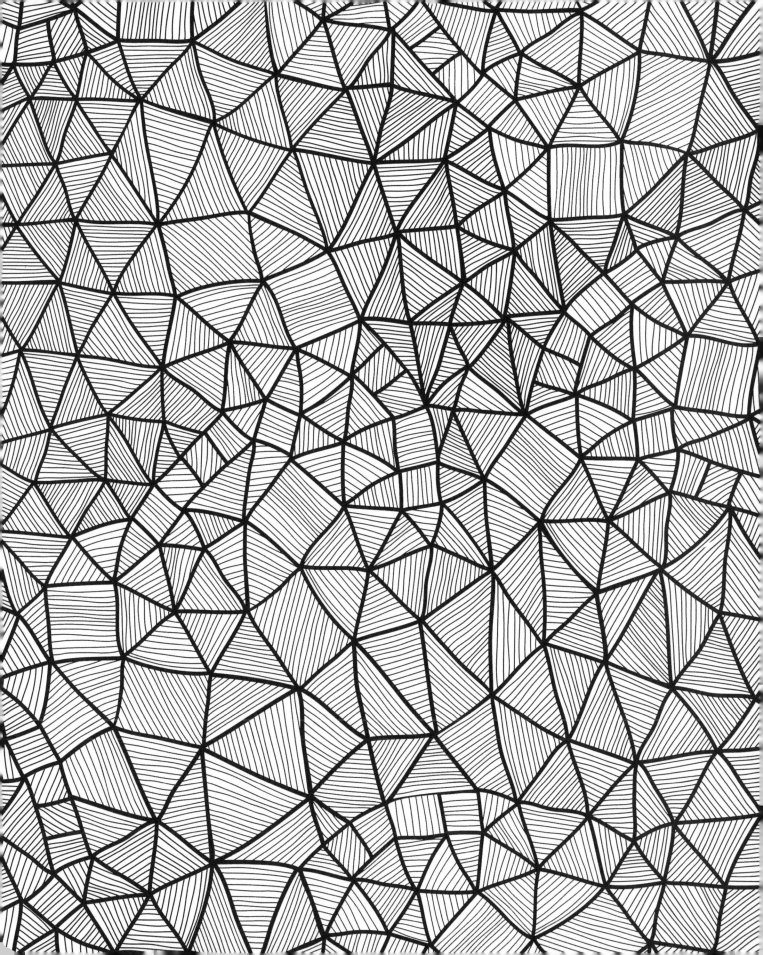

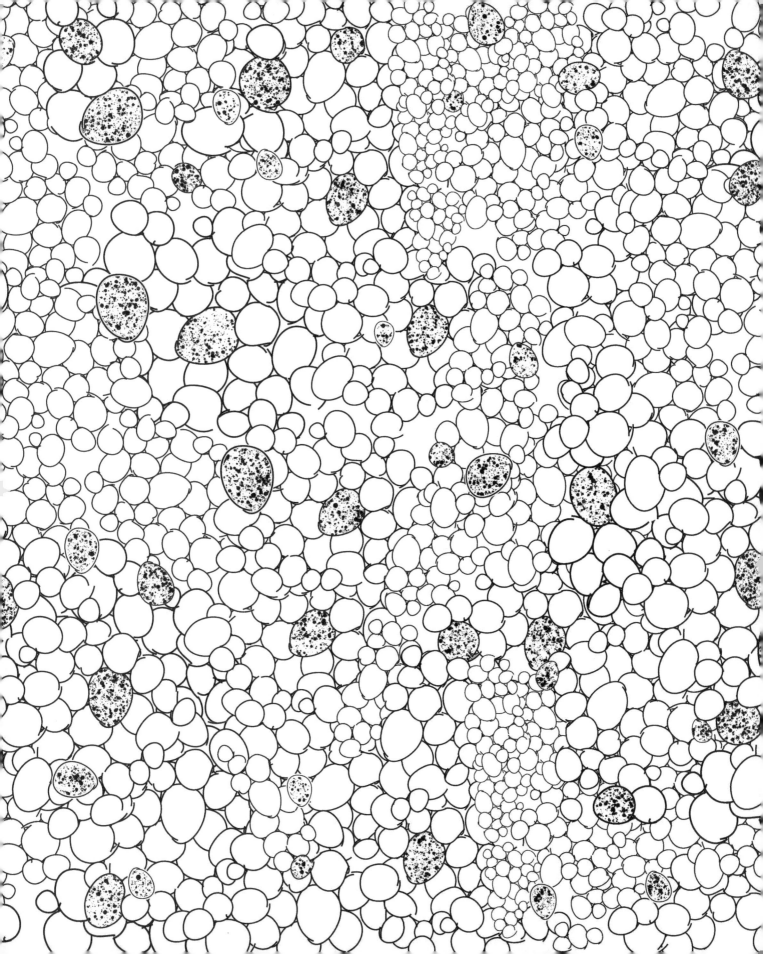

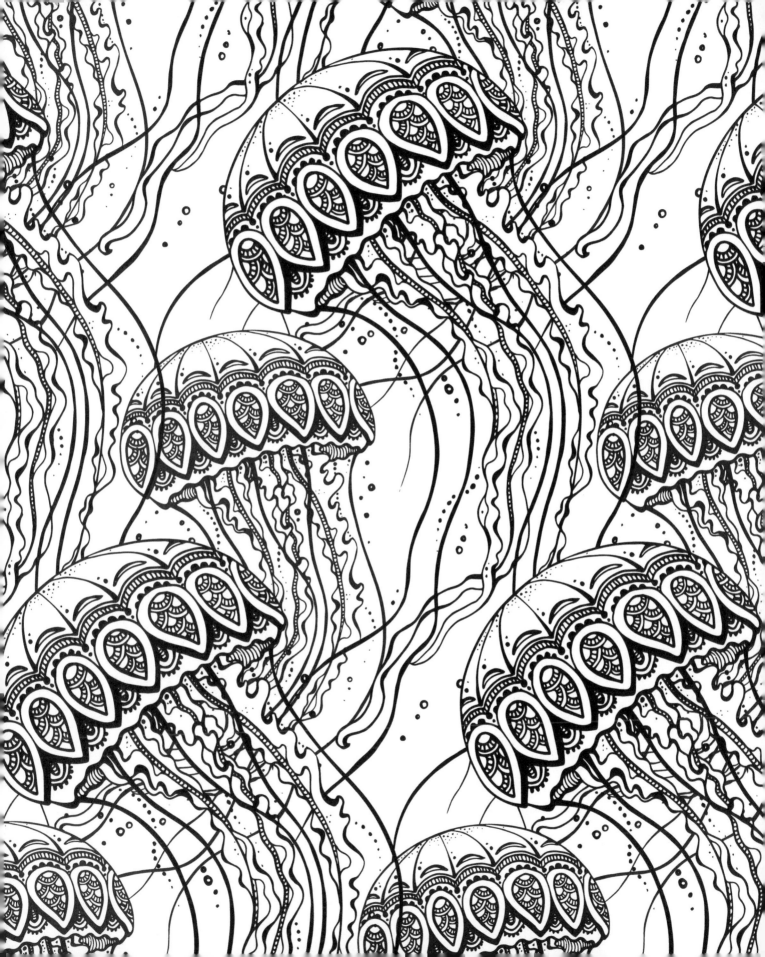

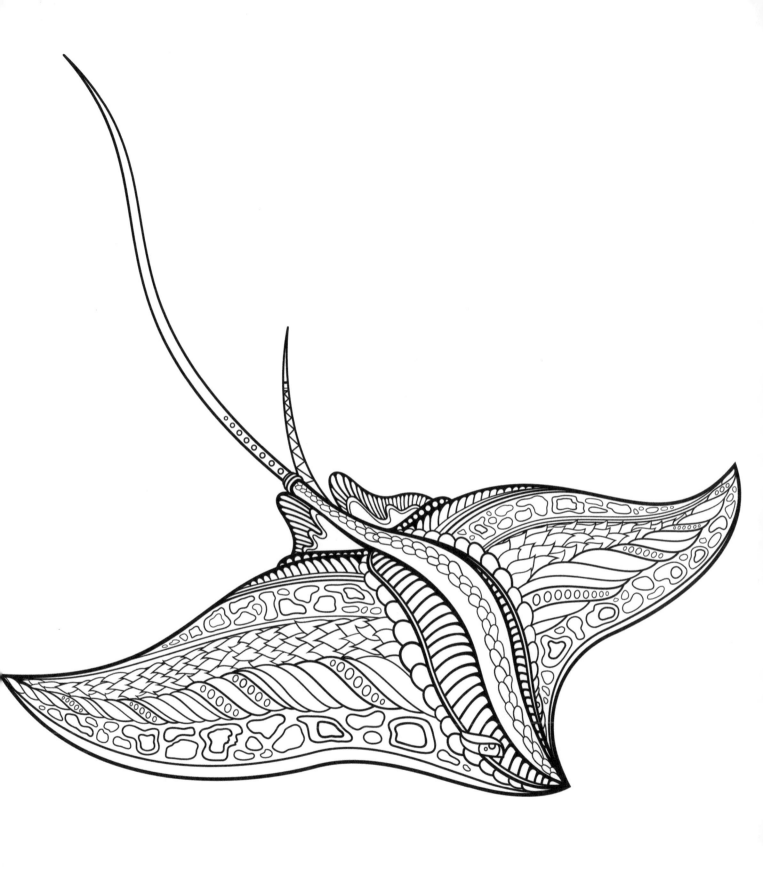

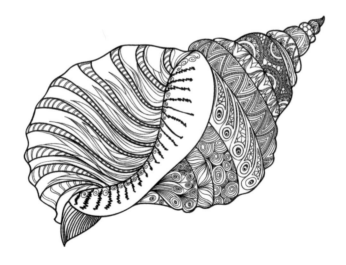

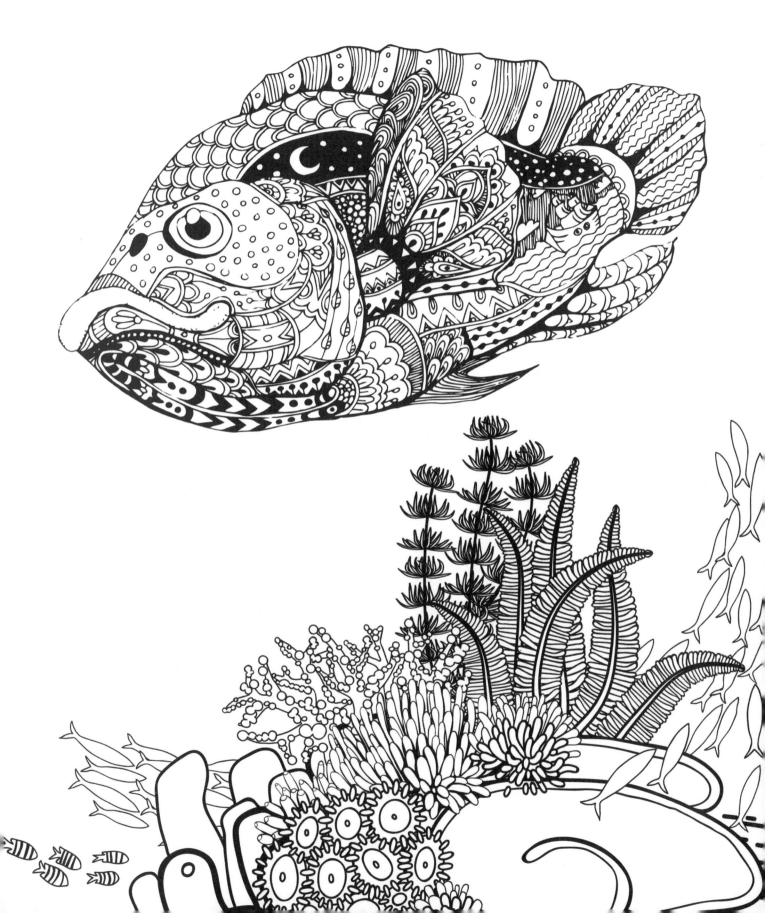

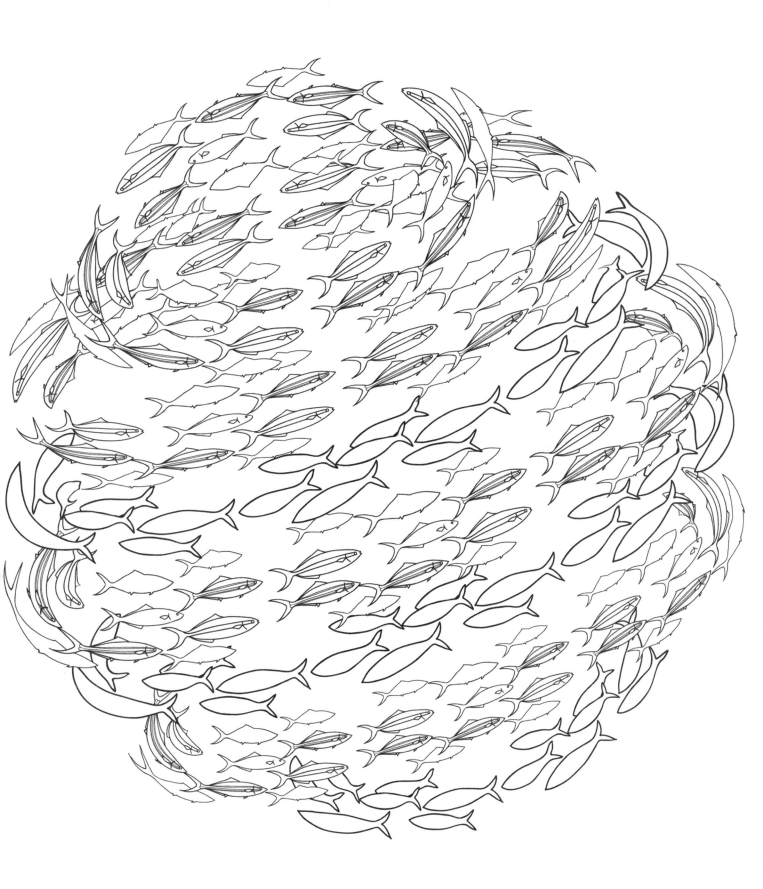

Everybody is a genius.

But if you judge a fish

by its ability to climb a tree,

it will live its whole life

believing that it is stupid.

ALBERT EINSTEIN

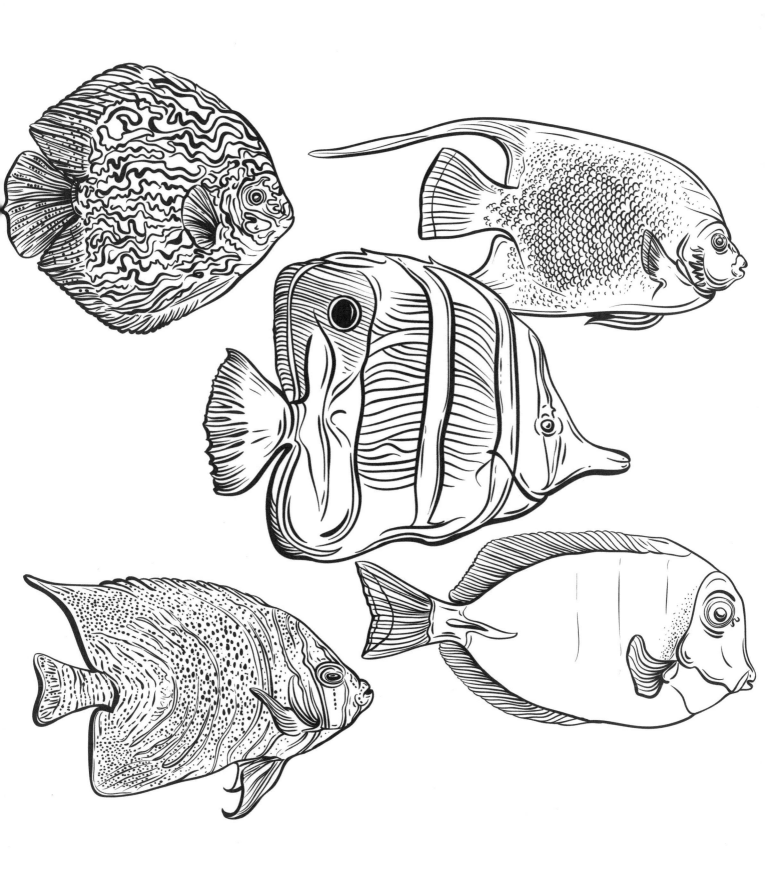

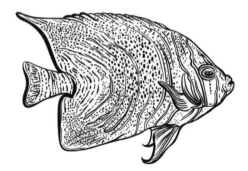